I SEE, HEAR & I CAN SPEAK

A Book of Empowerment

Yuki

Yuki's Art & Language

Gold Coast, Australia

DO I REALLY

HAVE WINGS?

Dedication to YOU and ME

Contents

QUANTUM LEAP TIME

The quantum levels of all things shift when metamorphosing takes place.

It is the natural law of cause and effect.

You may have hung onto the past until you bent your sacred tree to the max.

But now there is a chance to use that pressure by releasing it to fly high. All you need to do is let go.

It is time to free you from you.

Quantum Leap time

Past

I HAVE COME OUT OF THE WORLD I KNOW

If you have come out of the world you know, the world of the old way, then everything is different.

You have come out of the world you know, but you find that you are now okay. Not like how you were in fear in the old place.

So in this new world, breathe and be okay.

Life is okay.

Not like how you felt in the past.

It is more than okay.

It is incredible because you are free.

TEAR HAS BEEN SHED HERE

You may not have spoken up.

You may not have been heard.

You may not have been seen.

If so, the swelling heart got suppressed, and we have shed the tear inside.

If it comes out; if you can cry; then that's healthy.

These tears are waiting to come out of you because that's natural and healthy.

These tears have been watering your wishes.

If you have cried a lot, have a look; there is a field of beautiful creation within you.

Tear has been shed here

HERE

Open your hands and see the light from within.

Open your hands towards yourself and know that they are your gift to you. Those are tools for you to use.

Although these hands are for you, they also are you. The hands are a part of you.

It's just like how every one of us is a part of the whole, part of the source. We are 'One'.

And the awareness starts from here in your hands, in your heart, in your mind and your spirit.

You are powerful.

Embrace your hands, your heart, your mind and your spirit.

You are responsible for yourself.

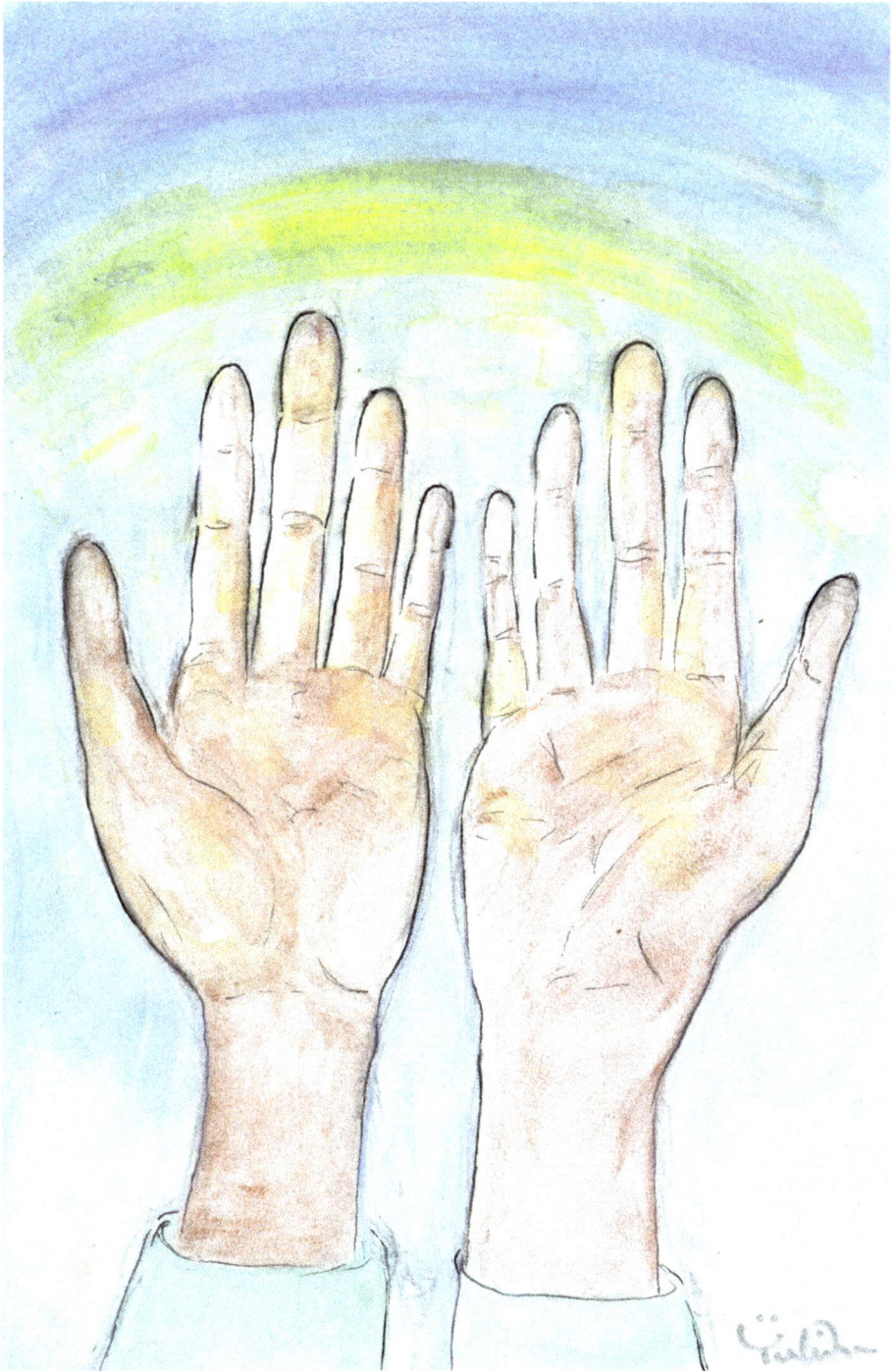

EMBRACE THE WHOLE SELF

Embrace the shadow and the light.

Don't just brush it off or suppress the shadow.

Acknowledge both the shadow and the light.

Embrace the whole self, as that is the authentic you.

When you integrate your shadow and light, the whole you can do magic. You can do anything when you are your whole self.

The whole self creates more and more.

As differences within you integrate, the whole self creates more stars continuously.

Integration produces a new star, a moment of joy and excitement in your life.

There's a meaning for the shadow and the light to be there for each other.

Embrace the whole self to be authentic.

BEHIND THE SET

I have made it to the back of the set.

I am in the hands of the ocean.

I've got a tool, a board to ride the waves.

I watch and breathe with the ocean, waiting for the divine timing, for I am ready to have the ride of my life.

I am here in the vast ocean.

Although the water is deep and relentless, it just feels so good to cleanse in this beautiful magnificence.

I am behind the set.

I am with the Ocean.

I am ready to ride the wave.

OUT OF CONTROL AT FIRST

Out of control at first.

But keep at it.

Get better at it and have fun.

Waves keep coming, but that's life's force.

Nature is in motion.

Nature has its flow.

So be aware.

Whether you ride the waves or not, there are no rests until you are out of the ocean.

That is the game of physical life.

EVERY STEP OF THE WAVE

The lotus flower sits on the water. As our awareness grows, the petals open one by one, eternally. This lotus never wilts nor stops blooming. Constantly expanding, this is our consciousness.

We obtain this wisdom only by experiencing life. By riding many waves and experiencing many layers of you.

Whatever way you take these rides; the overall picture is about the one long journey of getting to know you.

So enjoy the ride every step of the wave as much as you can.

Know that you came into this life for a good reason for yourself.

A SPARK OF IDEA

A spark of an idea can form as a concept and drop into your consciousness as a feeling.

If you notice it, ride it like a wave.

Sparks are like waves; they come and go.

You can see it, hear it and sense it when it comes.

Pay attention to your heart, as your heart is your guide.

Care for your heart enough to sense what feels right.

Carry your heart high to take off and hold your heart with you when you ride the waves.

Ultimately, that is the ride of a lifetime, and you can enjoy the ride of a lifetime every time!

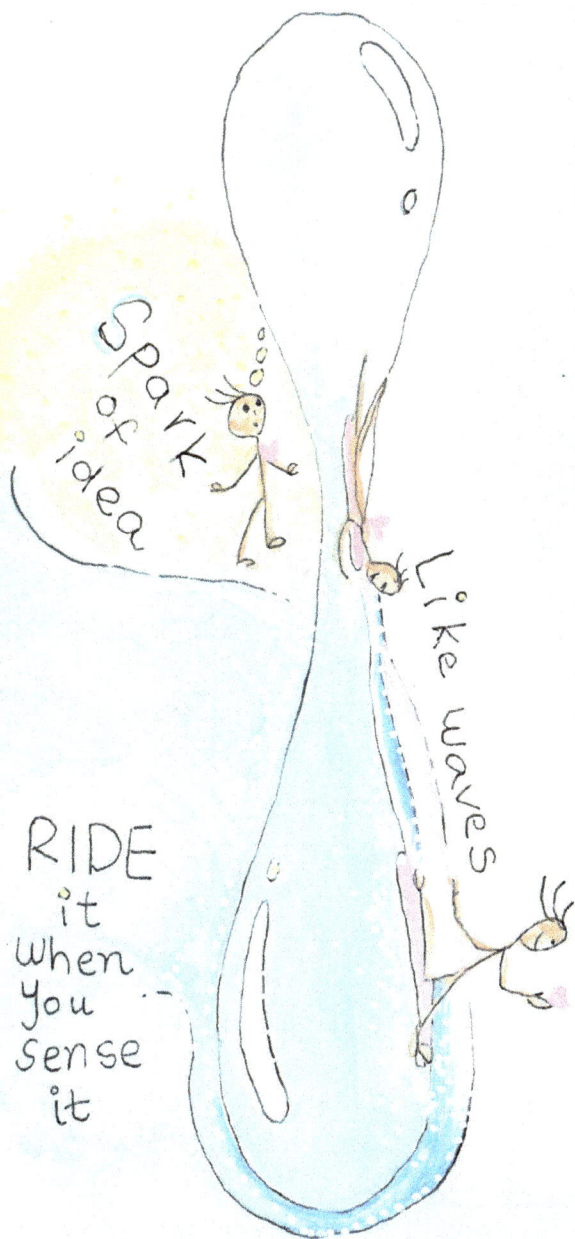

YES PLEASE, NO THANK YOU

It's okay to say no.

It's okay to say yes.

That is your free will and responsibility.

Keep finding out about yourself, what you like, what you don't like, what you accept and don't accept.

Drawing healthy boundaries is a way of promoting that you matter to yourself.

By doing this, you are creating your identity of who you are.

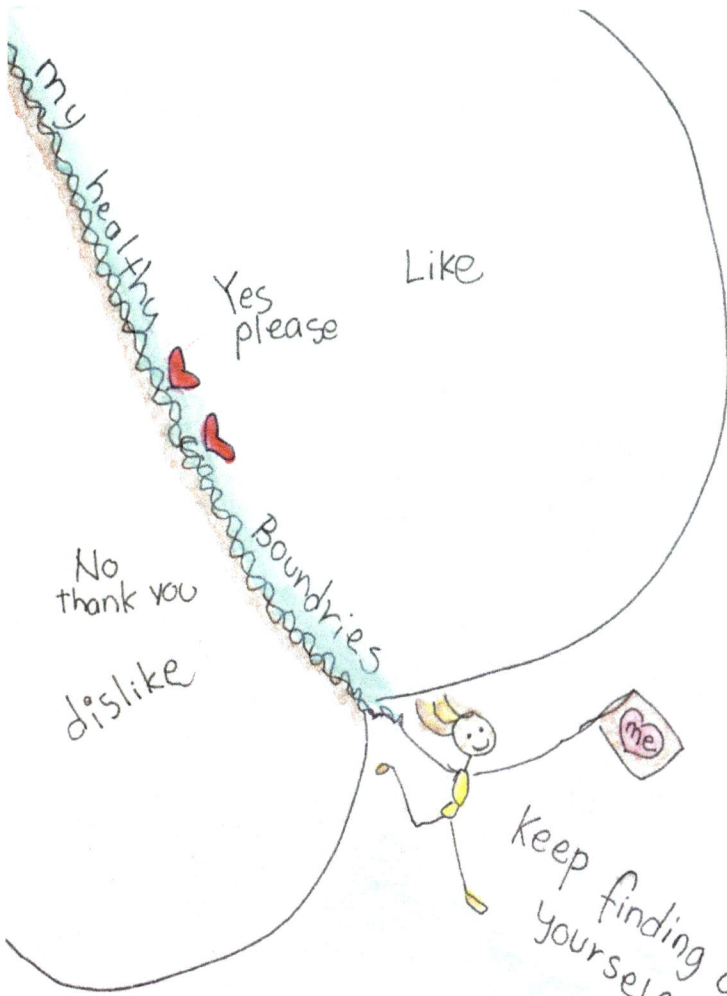

HOW DEEP IS THIS FEELING?

Take a look at the depth of your feelings.

Observing and understanding this feeling is key to your awareness.

Bring what has been subconscious to your consciousness by having a look.

Take your rose-colored glasses off so you can open your mind and seek the truth.

How deep is this feeling?

Can you peel off those layers one by one to recognize it?

There are so many layers to get to the original, the creation.

For we are multidimensional beings made up of so many layers.

When you take a look, you will realize how you are more significant than you think.

How deep is this
feeling?
separation
joy
fear
oneness
supression
self awareness
Self love
responsibility
Social Conditioning
Past lives
DNA/ancestry
Collective Consciousness
Cellular memory
Universal
Creation

PRESENT STAGE

There is no such thing as the past and the future.

Every moment we live, have lived or will live are in the present.

We are simultaneously living in it and observing it as our physical self and higher self.

So every moment is a stage show that you are watching.

Who are you in your show?

How are you playing your part in this present moment?

This present moment is the only place where we have the power to make choices and make a difference. It's the gift of time.

As you change the present, everything in the past, and potential future changes.

Present moments
of
Stage Shows

Who are you
& how are
you playing
your part?

potentiality

PRESENT

Past

for you
to see
watch
& observe

COME TO TERMS WITH IT

Sad things may have happened, and you may carry a necklace of tears.

There is a road of sadness that goes two ways, either forgiveness or an additional detour called destruction.

I choose it is time to come to terms with what has happened, as I have better things to do than be a victim to someone who doesn't care.

"I am not happy with what happened"... But what can I do now at this point in the aftermath?

I can take responsibility for my life now. I feel me. I listen to my feelings. I can then come to terms with my sadness, and that's a start.

Then, I can start my journey to get to the point of 'I am happy'.

A journey to forgiveness is a journey to freedom. And the ultimate destination is forgiving the self and being free from the sadness.

Come to terms with it.....

Road

← to →

forgivness

what can I do now?

I can take responsibility

of my life now

I feel me

I listen to my feelings

So I get to a point of

forgivness – it's a journey
...me...

FOOTSTEPS

Footsteps are the choices made in the world of free will.

Whether to live life being aware of that factor or not makes a difference in how you live your life.

A quantum physics experiment shows how electrons behave differently when we observe them to the time when we do not observe them. How does that work on a human when a person is observing oneself with conscious awareness?

See yourself walking in lively greenery, smelling the beautiful air and walking on solid ground.

You are in the light. You are living your life.

Your footsteps are lighting up with the life energy left from your feet, and the path you have taken illuminates.

Shining on all around you.

May you go on your journey in peace.

are
the
choices made in the
world of free will

YOU ARE THE ABSOLUTE POWER OF WHO YOU ARE

When you are not aware that you are the absolute power of who you are, you are creating chaos.

When you are not the leader of yourself, it's more than likely you are carrying baggage that does not even belong to you. And in that world, you are living in chaos. So look at yourself from outside of your self. Are you carrying others baggage? Are you living in chaos?

Know that no one can tell you how you should feel or what you should like and dislike.

Know that you are the absolute power of who you are.

Knowing this factor and being aware of who you are, creates your wish of peace and order.

You get to choose your path. Take responsibility for your own wellbeing as you have the absolute power of who you are.

Being aware creates your orders 🌱

ou
are
the
absolute
power
of
who
you
are ?

Not being aware creates chaos

MY WORLD IS MY CREATION

When you open your mind, you can see the egg you are holding in your arms. That is your world, your creation.

In the centre, your inner heart, your spirit and the flow of your life force reside. You are powerful when you know this.

Your heart is your wings.

You can walk on water if you can fly.

You can handle your own emotions if you are living authentically.

You can go beyond tears if you have a big heart that is your wings.

MY
world is
MY

CREATION

I am powerful

AS ABOVE SO BELOW, AS BELOW SO ABOVE

"I can show you how to jump."

"Show me how to jump."

Splash! Jump! Splash! Jump!

"Ha, ha, ah! It's so fun!"

"Yes, yes, yes, this is fun!"

A mama dolphin and a baby dolphin are living, sharing and caring for each other in the vast ocean of the physical world, the below.

Simultaneously, their kindred spirits are swimming around gently in their energy field from the above.

They are all synchronizing with the rhythm of life created from below with the above, above with the below.

It is as above, so below. It is as below, so above. It is a duality of the synchronized world.

All sides of us have symbiotic relationships.

As above
so below
As below
So above

HELLO MY HIGHER SELF

"Hello, hello my higher self". In our sleep, we meet again.

"I may forget you when I'm awake, but we do share the same dream, don't forget", I tell myself.

We meet up every night in our sleep.

"I am here for you through thick and thin. Let's hold our star together, our dream together" says my higher self.

"You may feel separated from me but I am never separate from you awake or asleep. I'm your higher self; your future self,"

...I hear you my higher self, echoing from deep inside like a dream. You are always with me.

Hello, my
higher self

A SOUL'S JOURNEY

Before being born, before taking the first breath, we existed in another form.

When we were in the astral world, we had a dream to have particular experiences in this physical life.

That is why we come into this world.

It is your dream that became this life force — you. It is your own choice to have this trip.

It was no one else's choice.

To complete a soul's journey... that is beyond just one life. We have gone on trip after trip. It is many lives, many wishes and dreams that we are carrying on to this current life.

This current life is extraordinary.

Find out why for yourself.

Yuki's Art & Language

www.yukisartandlanguage.com
@yukisartlanguage

Explore Your Potentiality
Discover who you are
Chose who you
want to become
It's your Life ⭐

www.ingramcontent.com/pod-product-compliance
Lightning Source LLC
Chambersburg PA
CBHW041823090426

42811CB00010B/1085